Dedication

The dedication of my first book can really only be given to one person. A multitude of people have given me inspiration in the writing of my poems and my wife who I love very much has supported me in the years it has taken to write this book and bring it successfully together. The person though who influenced me and introduced me to quirky style of Pam Ayres and Edward Lear also encouraged me to develop and use my imagination. In recognition of her love for me, I dedicate my first book to my Mum.

Contents

Chapter 1 – Love

Chapter 2 – Hate

Chapter 3 – Depression

Chapter 4 – Suicide

Chapter 5 – Christmas & Other Poems

Chapter 6 – Turkey

Chapter 7 – War

Chapter 8 – Auschwitz

Chapter 1 – Love

Love

Your eyes reflected the flames of love,

Your passion soared to new heights above.

Your majestic grace was evident to all,

Your royal line of love sounded a trumpets call.

As I bathed in your morning glow,

We moved together as one to the ebb and flow.

Like a bolt of lightning in a blue sky,

I would capture your tears whenever you'd cry.

We shared our love, a love oh so true,

That even paintings of landscapes spoiled the view.

I grew in your arms as you grew in mine,

A love that was shared, a love for all time.

Love Lost

Erstwhile glances of a cunning mind,

Across an ocean what can we find?

Crusoe's lot on an island view,

Heroes and Villains remind me of you.

One sail, two sails, three sails then four,

At my journeys end having voyaged o'er the floor.

Land Ho! Sighted, drop anchor and dock,

Time till we meet ebbs away tick tock.

Like cirrus high in a blue backed sky,

We embrace for our welcome then heave a sigh.

Never will I fall out or leave you alone,

You are my life, my love and my home.

Last Love

Hearts entwine for a final time,

Experiences learnt illuminate the sign.

Ball and chain and handcuffs to boot,

Heroes and Villains remind me of you.

Beautiful scenery passed along the way,

Tempting you not, all your life and a day.

Last love found time to live life to the full,

Happiness and content and love be your rule.

A Poem to Love

From the moment my eyes met yours my love was there,

Embracing you tightly at night then we'd share.

Awake in the morning bathing in our glow,

Body's intertwined, hearts pumping, breaths flow.

Love wants not waits together at last,

Single minutes in time forgetting the past.

Kisses and hugs join up to form a line,

Will you be my Valentine?

You My Diamond Blue

Lying in this aquatic paradise my thoughts surround you,

As the ocean crashes onto the land it reflects a diamond blue.

Its spray is all around me now churned up by the breeze,

And thoughts of you in diamond blue come gently and with ease.

I remember how we left it when you offered a sweet of lime,

Then I turned you down matter of factly cause I didn't have the time.

You looked a picture of Heaven in your costume by the sea,

Then words they did escape me so I wrote a poem of thee.

As I settled down in paradise and thought of things we'd do,

I wandered over to the sea again and remembered the diamond blue.

If I live to be a hundred I'll think of you every day of every year,

Then write some more poetry and wipe away that tear.

A Poem for a Woman.

I worked with you and eventually became your friend,

And now we're two ingredients in a very special blend.

You were as tall as I and your hair was very long,

Your eyes burned into my very soul as they met me through the throng.

A shiver sprinted down my spine and shook me to my very core,

Your embrace keeps me safe and comforts me when I'm sore.

Your voice is like a choir of the Heavenly Host,

And when you make me breakfast in bed you never burn the toast.

You and I are perfect together in each and every way,

And my love for you will continue to grow until my final day.

Chapter 2 – Hate

An untitled Poem by Me

I have awoken from my slumber, a heavy load with which I bare,

Unknown terrors in the night, my body sweats a lot to be fair.

I'm a product of my past and what a past my eyes have seen,

Not real anger or aggression like others have, but real enough for me.

A father sadistic and cruel who vented anger instead of love,

And turned me into an unfeeling zombie whose hand hit from above.

With low self-esteem and indifference to all, that has been insane,

My personal battles and wars have left a scarred cerebral plain.

Shell holes dot the landscape and black skies in the main,

The enemy of occupation has been vanquished to a degree.

But have left ticking time bombs to cause havoc or melee,

Casualties lie asunder stunted for eternity in their pain.

Child Abuse from every quarter, mummy and daddy unite as one,

Physical, emotional and covert inflict results as if for fun.

Though these happenings to a child might be forgotten in a day,

I am unfortunate not to be that child and will stay beside me in every way.

Daddy he did beat me as mummy watched to play the dutiful wife,

But kept her feelings hidden til he left and I caught strife.

Beaten with a stick and a rail and thrown down the stairs,

Shouting, roaring, smacking, throwing remote controls it really scares.

Suicidal thoughts and attempts to stab myself in bed,

My brother left this hellish life before it pickled his head.

Controlled by love on one side of the coin and terror on the reverse,

My life is now in the hands of a tablet to keep my demons immersed.

Food suppresses feelings but thoughts of old fill me in a furore,

With thoughts to kill now prominent of my parents to heal the sore.

This would not cure me though, but temporary relief would appear,

But greater conscience pricking for decades will result but not a tear.

They will reap the fruits of their labour, to this I have no doubt,

As their enemy forces are beaten back as one greater forces a rout.

On their swords they will fall and a shout will go up to the sky,

But I will not be in attendance though I'll know but never cry.

A Prayer of a Killer

Whisper softly, lay you down to sleep,
Pull the scarf tighter don't make a peep.
Soft in my arms getting lighter of life,
Less of a struggle no use for a knife.

Lie on the ground now my baby blue,
Sleep baby sleep no harm to hurt you.
You passed on arousal as your energy surged,
I thank you so much the result was purged.

Escape now I must so I bid you farewell,
Sleep peacefully for now no one will I tell.
Finding you again will our bodies then lie,
My love assured I will see in your eye.

Never let us part or argue the toss,
If ever you leave I will feel a loss.
So let me toast our future together in life,
Never to die my already dead wife.

Anger

Black clouds gather the sky turns dark from blue,

Pressure mounts, eruption is imminent, and language starts to spew.

Momentary lull for a question, before action, word and deed,

Pressure surge multiplied by a million and ejaculates at speed.

Falling boulders, shards of debris come cascading to the ground,

Loved ones or pets or belongings lie injured all around.

A pyroclastic flow of flaming words continue to achieve,

Scars in relationships that will harden, without relief.

Energy spent and damage done, plunge into a despair so deep,

Cutting skin on broken glass is a release and result not to weep.

Rise of the Phoenix flames to stoke the fire, temperature almost met,

Rumble in the clouds that gather again to repeat without regret.

<u>To Whom It May Concern</u>

You're only remembered for the last good thing you do,

Nobody ever remembers the good deeds now they're out of view.

Remember I bought you all of those gifts and entertained in my free time?

No you don't and that's just terrible in fact it's just a crime.

You didn't do that work and had ran out of time til my expertise blew you away,

You took it in the next day and without me, you wouldn't have gotten an A.

Always unconditional and with glee to be your favourite was my itch,

But low and behold I'm not to you, instead to me you're just a bitch!!!

Chapter 3 – Depression

A Short Poem of Life

Ebb and flow of life and love,

Like an albatross in the skies above.

Lonely figures in darkened clouds,

Lonely birds in darkened shrouds.

Many a year from sounds of life,

Many a year in silent sight.

Turning, soaring, flying, crying,

Birds of light and in darkness, death.

The Ship

As the ship rocked and rolled in the swell,

Of sailor's courage, the shanty songs would tell.

What fate which ebbed closer would they meet?

To Davy Jones' locker was only 5 feet.

Just then the waves broke over the bridge,

And to the port stood a lighthouse on a ridge.

Flashing its light on the danger ahead,

An Ensign got the Captain out of bed.

Valiantly he urged the ships rudder to turn,

As coal was shovelled into the boilers to burn.

But as she wallowed in her now impending doom,

Onto the rocks her fate now did loom.

The men fought to turn her away,

But success escaped them as did another day.

Not once nor twice but thrice they urged,

To no avail towards the rocks the ship surged.

Devoid of hope and of families now to dream,

They listened in horror to the ships dying scream.

With the force of the sea onto the rocks she ploughed,

This once mighty tanker of oil was endowed.

Lashed by the waves she rolled onto her side,

And all the brave men at their stations had died.

Remembered forever on a cenotaph by the sea,

Not forgotten in song by sailors like me.

Happy Birthday to Me

It was 41 years ago when I was born in a city with
strife,
It was not the fashion for my father to attend leaving it
all to his lowly wife.

It had started with a thought then an egg,
heartbeat, an eye, ear or a leg.
Like Patrick Duffy I lived in a sea,
breathing water wasn't alien to me.

On 1st October 1971 I arrived,
Out I came as the contractions contrived.
Cleaned and wrapped up breast feeding was a joy,
This act would later shape her baby boy.

Through schools into adulthood I was a freak,
Looking back I can only think "EEK."
Meeting my Wife is where my life had begun,
Having continued to stay healthy and run.

Now I'm aged 41 and it's gone fast,
And my dice have all but been cast.
I'm older now and will continue to be,
Never younger until a cure finds me.

Me Myself and Me

All alone in a sea of many,

Thoughts of self and not of many.

Self-implosion and no self-worth,

Worship of fears and not of mirth.

Life of a clown filled with lies,

Belly of laughs coupled with sighs.

Filling a gap of depression and fear,

Wipe away the sad solitary tear.

Thoughts of suicide nothing but alone,

No truths to ponder only lies to atone.

Darkness abounds in my shadow world,

Praise to the dark clouds demons unfurled.

No end in sight or end of this terror,

Nothing to see or return from a mirror.

Just the awful sight of a dead man alive,

To the end never to finish but continue to deprive.

Life

Thought inspiring words once came from a song that was written,

Words that had a profound impact leaving me totally smitten.

By a man called Kris Kristofferson this song his hand wrote,

"He was a walking contradiction", was the amazing quote.

Like the big guns report that signalled the start of a battle,

The cogwheels in my mind began to shudder and rattle.

I had wandered this land for 40 years now unknowing who I was,

A bolt of lightning had me thinking before a pause.

What if Kris was right and he had written that for me,

What land is this we live in what can special people see?

Or maybe it was for another and I'm a little loose in the head,

A little short of sense or just easily lead.

But in the end is there a "truth" sent to confuse and jam,

Exactly who I'd like to be or who I really am?

Maybe I'm just a nobody sent to walk upon this earth,

With no real sense of anything or even any self-worth.

A Ballad of Self Pity

To get to know the person that is the Poet Darren Paul,

Then gather round and listen and we'll start when he was small.

He wasn't very significant though in height he was quite tall,

He never joined in with other boys when they played football.

His mummy loved him very much and smothered him all the time,

He liked to read the works of Pam Ayers funny rhyme.

Edward Lear was another of her favourites that he really got to like,

He never really played with kids and rode solitarily on his bike.

When it was time to go to school he didn't know how to act,

And even threw sand in a boy's eye, now that's a fact.

Reading quietly was his form in classrooms full of noise,

Then get beaten up at playtime by a gang of ignorant boys.

All through school he tried to pass and get in by a nose,

Then disappear into the throng as leaders fell and rose.

He got 4 C's in subjects were he should have gotten an A,

But speaking out in class was not what he would say.

So into the big bad world our hero sprang one day,

Old habits didn't die in him and still he wouldn't play.

Leaving jobs after only a few days was a coat that began to fit,

Even his family took bets on whether he'd stay or sit.

Finally after many years and many tears he's in a job that he enjoys,

And you wouldn't ever believe it but he plays with the other boys.

He has a beautiful wife, big house and two cars in the drive,

A forward looking approach now to a very happy life.

Time to Eat

The clock ticked and tocked in time,

The eyes flickered and read the rhyme.

The pages turned keeping pace and all was fine,

The poets' words were eaten in their prime.

But the clock still ticked as the pendulum swung,

The eyes still ate the words as it continued and had done.

The pages turned in unison gathering speed not for fun,

As the poets words were eaten not leaving a crumb.

The words became like letters posted into a greedy brain,

No let up or quarter given reading forward not to refrain.

Fast approached the ending, mind power in the wane,

Until another book is laid down for a lunch to start again.

An Ugly Duckling

From an urge to an egg then a surge into life, on
unsuspecting world,

From early years and crying tears, from a mother a
bird emerges.

Flight from the nest is never easy, a mothers control
can make it quite queasy,

The strength to fly away, the weakness to stay is a
sway.

With continuous arbitration life dries up with
starvation,

To suckle with a mother who controls and means to
smother.

How much longer can a bird survive with an
overprotective cover,

Never feeling what life is like until a nose dive sends it
over.

Down to the earth it fell with a bang, the angels fell
too as they sang,

Oh glory to life and its joy after 23 years it's a boy.

The bird had to make its own mistakes living in the long grass among the snakes,

A life of ordinary loves heartache, trouble and peace like the doves.

It could fly with considerable ease experiencing life it could laugh and tease,

To a group of hidden talents it fitted in with suitable requirements.

The bird found a love for life to share with a Gazelle that flew in the air,

In a life so complete at last, it was a stark contrast.

For them both life would be good, living it for eternity, the way they should,

The duck had now become a swan, through tribulations came a bright new dawn.

Depression

Jets propel across the sky,
As I sit here asking my life why?

In a room that is myself I am told,
Dank walls, no light and very cold.

Encased and forgotten for many a year,
Dry your eyes and don't shed a tear.

T'was my fault that I am locked away,
No confidence to go outside and play.

Trapped in a world of an untamed beast,
My survival is uncertain to say the least.

Hiding away I fall into a sleep,
No friends to help no quest I seek.

Having lived in solitude for many a while,
I'll walk with me for eternity's mile.

Married to my partner that is now my room,
'Til I reach an end and embrace my doom.

Chapter 4 – Suicide

Suicide Note

Some people love the sunshine while others like me love the rain,

Some people relish their loved ones while others like me embrace the pain.

I'm inconsolably lonely as I have no friends of which to speak,

And for eternity in a trough destined to never reach a peak.

Why would anyone love me? What is there present for all to see?

Run fast away and leave me to solitary thought were I'm free.

I am disappointed by people in all they say and do,

I have known oh so many and respected but a few.

Liars, deceitful freaks and geeks, gangsters, thieves and deviants that I knew,

Tie them altogether and a strange bunch of persons I am this is true.

So here I am ready to die beckoning the end as on my bed I lie,

With no one left to love me and no one who cares enough to say goodbye.

To Seek the End

Slide the brass into the chamber,
Snap it shut now ready to fire.
Pull the trigger nerves don't waver,
Pull the trigger now not a liar.

Here the fall of the hammer,
Then the pin to oblivions ride.
Nothing happens, no report, no explosion,
No retort, check the slide.

Eject the round and start again,
Ease the barrel to the head.
No need to aim and ready to fire,
Pull the trigger now you're dead.

Or maybe not as pain flows in,
Can't remember not to do it again.
Hole through the temple brain too thick,
Slowed the bullet not so simple.

Here I lie in a vegetable state,

Cannot think, hear, love or hate.

Just growing old in this bed I lie,

Not quick to live but slow to die.

Bitter Pill

The leaves turned red I've been shot but not dead,

My love for you is alive and true like the poet said.

They tried to break that which we had,

But what we have is definitely no fad.

So with a bullet they tried to remove,

My love for you that I had to prove.

Their lust is a feeling and not trust,

To give succour would only breed fuss.

Nothing lives in their barren land,

Only in love between a woman and man.

So I will rest and recover some more,

If it wasn't love it wouldn't be sore.

They thought they'd win with overkill,

Our unknown strength to live was their bitter pill.

To fight for your beauty in mine,

To live long and survive for all time.

Life is Death

Here I am alone in my life,

Hushed quiet in reverend tone.

Play in my world as I stay in my room,

Life dies slowly in this comfortable tomb.

No one to live for or strive to succeed,

Dry away tears heart starts to bleed.

Isolated in love unrequited or none,

Cutting wrists not for fun.

Immersed in my dreams unsure of what's real,

Black clouds gather like a heavenly veil.

Suffocate, starve, cut or hang,

Answers provided with a bullet and bang.

Care Not for Me

For all of you who know me or know of to tell the truth,

Care not a thought for my wellbeing for I would never sooth.

I think of you all mostly never and remember the names of but a few,

I'm wrapped up in my own importance though self-worth has gone askew.

Babies are born and children achieve though mothers pride holds nothing in me,

I care not for your petty lives so I ask, care not for me.

Love your lives and gather mementoes placing pictures on your wall,

Darkness adorns my living space as I don't care for any of you at all.

Future lives sound wonderful as everyone fills up with joy,

My life continues aimlessly and being rude has become my only toy.

As your lives open up with joyous rapture waste not your hopes to send,

For you have made your life to be lived and I've made mine to be at an end.

Chapter 5 – Christmas & Other Poems

Christmas Time

It was cold and wet on that Israeli plain, here the locals awoke with much distain,

Romans ruled as Zealots looked on forlorn, unknowing the Christ had been born.

A saviour for their lives but not in their way, after 33 years they'd make him pay,

For the present he was a gift to all and like a baby did crawl, cry and fall.

In the 2000 years since the birth of our King, man perverted this to a money thing,

No longer a celebration for a child, it's a disgusting display and a memory defiled.

So how can we make a return to the old and reinvigour the story we were told,

Let's make greed and gluttony a crime and ring out the bells for Christmas time!!

Life as it is Part 1

It was a cold and misty morning as the trumpets began to wail,

The Heavenly Host was gathering in strength to face its Demonic foe.

And on that amazing land, the sights and sounds and shit got real.

God was there in shimmering white with Jesus and the Archangels abreast,

His Angels stood to attention in their divisions numbering too many to count.

As far as you could see was his army laden and ready to fight and not test.

The Prince of Darkness stood opposite with his own Angels and hordes from hell,

Rising to the challenge they screamed obscenities at the Royal Household.

A fight to the death was in the offing this day, who'd win only time would tell.

For 7 days and 7 nights battles raged across the Heavenly Plain,

Searching for a weakness up and down each Army's lines.

To the death with no quarter given, hard fought battles did not refrain.

First it was Raphael then Gabriel before Michael exploited an ill disciplined foe,

Flashes of lightning emanated from the swords of the Demonic force.

God's shock troops widened the breach into which his forces did go.

Lucifer's forces were in full flight as Heaven rebuked them at every turn,

Decimated and routed the once grand demonic army looked for a place to hide.

But nowhere was a safe haven as one by one their fortresses did burn.

Captured collectively and lead away in chains went the motley crew,

Judgement came upon them as their loyalty was not for God.

Towards an eternity of pain and nightmares for Satan's service would they imbue.

And so it was that peace reigned after that war that was now won,

God sent his son to earth to save mankind for Himself.

But Satan's demons distorted man for his own ends and goal number one.

Deafness

Solitary sounds lost on searching ears,

A world of silence surrounded by fears.

To never hear leaves rustle or birds cheep,

Enjoy affection as your wife does speak.

Alone in a world still foreign and new,

Where nobody lives but memories and you.

When deafness came to envelope your life,

An involuntary motion of pain and strife.

You didn't ask for it and welcomed it not,

But arrive it did and cared not a jot.

Housed in your head and here to stay,

On holidays, birthdays at rest and at play.

Towards a reduced future of silence you walk,

Learned studies later your hands will talk.

Taking your place in a world so new,

No sound, just silence with sights left to view.

Bun Shop

Cream Buns, Cakes, Rolls, Flans, Tray Bakes, Biscuits and Apple Tart,

Around the shop I stare and around the shop my eyes dart.

Which one will be my selection or how many shall I have?

Can I get them home in time before I think I'll starve?

As I bite down into an iced finger the cream oozes out over my lips,

As for that glass of fat coke, I will have to drink in sips.

Guzzling down each sugar filled slice and every tasty piece,

Maybe working in a bakery is where I'll find my niche.

I imagine wakening up and going to work in sugar heaven,

Or if I had the money, I'd buy a sugar house to live in.

Back down to reality with a bump I come after my sugar rush has gone,

So it's off down to the bun shop again I hope they never move on.

The Night They Ransomed Christmas.

It was an eve in December as the people slept in their
beds,
When a dastardly plan was hatched and it formed in
evil heads.

For the ruination of Christmas was the goal of the
forlorn few,
Who plotted to steal the innocence from the children
they never knew.

And so a letter was sent to the Mayor in the sleepy
town,
With far reaching consequences for all and sundry
found around.

Of such a shock to all who read it and could not begin
to understand,
The reasons and the why fors searched solutions
from this man.

He called together church men from each concerned
community,

And asked for honest opinions delivering suggestions with impunity.

No one could decide which way was best to spoil this demonic cause,
Nor stop the leaks to an outside world who react without pause.

He tried to stop the Broadcasters and the Papers from going to print,
He wanted a stay of execution so as not to lose a mint.

As the clocks ticked fast and time ran on with nowhere left to run,
He called on all world leaders for a summit on what was to be done.

As the talking started in earnest with Emissaries Eager to Please,
No one had a clue what to do and ended up trying to appease.

The problem seemed unsolvable as it meant more than just money,

It went to the heart of what we believe is Santa real or just a phony.

The innocence of all the children was at stake that night,
As the Intellectuals and wise men began to shout and start to fight.

While the punches flew a young man stood up at the back,
And addressing the Mob he hit the table with a Whack.

The answer is simple he said as he held his hands up to the sky,
It isn't Rocket Science or Algebra but a solution he did cry.

No matter what the ransom is it's a sum that we all must pay,

For all children must continue to believe till they mature someday.

To rob them of this would essentially kill off their imagination,
And that terrible day would be oh so much a tribulation.

So if this is not the last time but the start of a regular claim,
Then the Mayor must act by himself or else suck up all the blame.

And so it transpired that the gang was paid and the children never knew,
Christmas then came and went so fast it made the Mayor whistle Phew.

The secret was to remain in a safe guarded with a lock and a key,
To remain untouched for eternity it was locked not once or twice but three.

So days grew into weeks and then months and not
even a peep was heard,

Then November arrived with a silence that deafened
but not a word was dared.

As the world held fast of its breath the result was a
visual interpretation,

The stock markets fluttered with extreme dismay that
caused a recorded vibration.

In the end it had all been for nothing as the world
sighed with total relief,

The alarm although now over had been intense but
remarkably brief.

As peoples thoughts turned to a Happy New Year
filled full of good cheer,

The dawn beckoned a new era of innocence without
caution, contempt or fear.

Chapter 6 – Turkey

Through a Woman's Eye

Why are some men so different from the rest?

Like I'm an interviewing host and they're the guest?

We live together, eat together, sleep together and play!

But really they are empty shells, shallow and vacant all day!

Holidaying in the sun like other couples having fun.

They lie there like logs, lifeless and tanning in the sun!

Why do I stay when these dogs do not resemble other men?

Am I stuck in a rut or is this going to be the trend?

Is my knight in shining armour really a dream or is this a test?

Should I look above the seconds and only accept the best?

Turkey by the Sea

Boiling sun above me and around me the people are thin,

The critters on this molten landscape try digging themselves in.

Shingle, stone and sand in this place are to be found,

Lying here too long a day, you'll find you've over browned.

Waves crash down asunder while foam forms in their wake,

People stand around or lying, sun creams ready then they bake.

Two weeks or less in this oven and they'll be brown like a little bun,

Too much heat or not enough can make or break their fun.

And so it comes to pass with every landing plane,

That takes the bakers produce away and home again.

Everyone needs a little sunshine to brighten up their life,

Or else all work and no play will stress and twist the strife.

So save up all that hard earned money and fly out to Turkey,

Were the locals are really friendly and the water isn't murky.

Billowy it can be and hot it can also sometimes be,

But come on out and look for yourselves, come on you'll see.

Under the Sea

If I could live underwater just think how that'd be,

Four big domes of living room, with a view out to the sea.

Whether wakening up or going to sleep, no curtains would I need,

I could play my music very loud and annoy no one indeed.

Swim with the fish and spear them with the aid of an aqua lung,

Then cook up a culinary delight that was tasty on the tongue.

Having friends round to visit would be an amazing sight,

Think about not having to clean or tidy . . . yeah right!

Going to the shops would be easy Tesco's could drop it in a chest,

Scuba Dive out to get it, hook up the sea horses and they'll do the rest.

Yes an underwater life would be a dream come true at last,

But that's about all it'd be because my wife wouldn't let it past.

Chapter 7 – War

Reflections

Lying there still and crest fallen, thoughts of defeat,

A battle is lost, a wars end it does wreak.

The butchery, the slaughter and the bleeding has stopped,

Though the guns have fallen silent, dead bodies still rot.

Tangled, disfigured and frozen in time, their souls now at peace,

Death hides the horror, with rolling mists, in they race.

A blight and a scar of society's anger and rage,

Will men now pause and of wars dissuade?

Bright eyed boys and in months enemies were,

Now lying at peace with each other and at each other they stare.

A tumultuous event had happened and left them there to lie,

Hands no longer move, heart stopped, eyes don't cry.

The years have gone by since the great battle went wrong,

Ground is now repaired and awoken by bird song.

The trees stand tall to attention like men,

Hoping for peace and not war again.

Destruction!!!

Tears trickle, thoughts race, pain subsides and men relent,

How could they do such a horrid thing to release the beast from hell sent.

Profound apologies to a world of the old,

To a blackened shell and a story not yet told.

The missiles rained down from the sky above,

They came to kill not filled with love.

And so it was over, that no man could withstand,

A burned out, desolate, beautiful land.

Nuclear Holocaust

The sun shone and the wind blew and adorning the
grass was the morning dew,

Broken windows, tattered blinds, streets silent without
a clue.

Ash on the living room floor,

A hole were once was a door.

No sign of life in a world gone bad,

Nothing left living or able to feel sad.

A push of a button, flash of light to exhaust,

No more stockpiles only Nuclear Holocaust.

In Life and Death

Seeds planted in a row by division,

Are split after the collision.

Growing with the aid of water and light,

Forming a body with a head that's right.

Transferred to pots that nurture and protect,

Gazing up from a cradle with time to reflect.

Producing a growth into plant hood they go,

Crawling then walking, putting on a show.

Moved to a forest, metal fences keep safe,

Children they play mixed together is brave.

Perils of life, fire burns all around,

Cut knees or breaks when they fall to the ground.

Round the corner sees older trees full of leaves,

First days of work, happy days do you believe?

Branches sway to and fro, leaves fall bark grows,

Birthdays, weddings, funerals, life's breath blows.

Invaded by fungus on the frontline we find,

Brother against brother that's war, friends find.

Looking back at the young tree's memories adrift,

Open fire, heating cold toes, death comes swift.

Ashen logs smoulder, life ebbs away,

Entombed forever in the ground were they'd lay.

Hunger

Children Larked in the playground as the birds flew overhead,

No emotion in those eyes, only a look both dark and dead.

Soaring in formation across the sky, no engines made a sound,

Towards their destination in one direction they were bound.

At last the leader dipped his wing and headed for the deck,

Followed by his squadrons aiming for bread to peck.

No bombs, death or disaster in this poem as you can see,

Just some hungry little birdies finding a meal eventually.

Chapter 8 – Auschwitz

<u>The Abyss</u>

Since I've come to hell in Auschwitz and had a look in
Pandora's Box,
I'm travelling home to Larne and can't wait to wash
and detox.

Since seeing all the horror and with my gift I heard the
screams,
They permeate my mind and invade all my dreams.

In my throat there's grown a lump that makes me
want to be quite sick,
It started in my stomach and how it'll pass will be the
trick.

With the smell of hospital chlorine in the rooms that
shouldn't be,
The hills of shoes and pots belonging to the free.

Wire spectacles in a heap that looks like wire wool,
Rusted knives and spoons lie around in the mud like
a discarded tool.

The victims of this genocide have long since passed
away,
Their souls don't want to leave though it's here they
want to stay.

Around the Crematoria and the Gas Chambers no
birds sing,
No sound is heard at all now no not ever not a thing.

Selection

The train door opened quickly and made a deafening
sound,
Lights awash us everywhere dogs barking, soldiers
shouting all around.

Into the lines we went, families separated for the first,
Sounds of children screaming the Nazi's will be
cursed.

The doctors looked us over and selected just a few,
The rest continued down the road to where no one
knew.

"Papa where are you going?" "Where is Mama in the
din?"
Picked up by a stranger to the shower blocks carried
in.

The Guards said, "have a wash now and don't forget
behind your ears,"

"Then clean your dirty face and dry up all those tears."

"You'll want to be all clean when you get your uniform,"
"There's nothing to be afraid of this really is the norm."

Standing under the showers we find and all the taps are turning,
Though as we turn them harder, water is not then forthcoming.

A heightened state of panic begins to rear its ugly head,
That terror scream of death is all that can be said.

Holes appear in the ceiling gas canisters dropping in,
Doors are closed and lights go off slow deaths now begin.

The smell of fear hangs heavy above the smell of gas,
Throughout the block it spreads now it's everywhere at last.

Nails torn of fingers digging helplessly against the wall,
Packed in tightly like sardines we couldn't even fall.

Urine and faeces are everywhere lungs labour for a breath,
Black silence reaches out to my soul and takes it with my death.

So what became of my body was I buried in the ground?
No all there was to greet it was the flames licking all around.

With gold fillings pulled from my teeth and wedding ring off my finger,
My body's joined the others in the oven 'cause they weren't allowed to linger.

Never Stay in Auschwitz.

If you ever visit Auschwitz It's okay to have a look,
But don't ever think of staying the night leave quickly like a crook.

An overbearing dead weight is applied to all who stay the night,
And staying more is madness or so I found all right.

Within those walls the unspeakable happened and has infected everything,
The funeral pyres have cast the ash in the direction the wind would bring.

The people look and stare with empty eyes in your direction,
Laughter doesn't exist here and joyous sounds have no selection.

Is it because of Auschwitz's torrid past that has left things as they seem,
Or has the stench from Hell's Abyss intoxicated all who dream.

While I stayed I could feel the sorrow of the innocents who cried beneath,
And driven to distraction by the screams that they bequeath.

Who are they I hear you ask though I know you'll call me mad,
They are some of those who were slaughtered and who are now very bad.

The spirits of the dead who are out to even the score,
Entered my own searching mind and downloaded all the gore.

I touched the walls in the Death Block and hellish pictures first drew blood,
Then stood at a darkened cell door and vivid images became a flood.

Then standing very still with my back to the firing wall,
I saw the guns and heard the screams and saw the innocents fall.

Past the wire of death I touched the electric fence,
The images they grew clearer and I saw the faces
hence.

They looked at me in fear and began to scream
aloud,
Then all went black as if under a deathly shroud.

I closed my eyes to see their secret worlds inside,
Replaying over and over my thoughts I cannot hide.

No one saw those faces and the screaming they
would make,
Still tortured in the afterlife and torturing me now for
goodness sake.

So I said my goodbyes to Auschwitz and those faces
from the past,
Heading home to Larne with dark memories that
would last.

How will I put these pictures of my adventure to a
rest?
And go forth in my life again to rationalise and digest.

When I see injustice happening in whatever form it
makes,
I will do my level best to snuff it out before it takes.

In memory of those dead and gone and the suffering
that became,
I swear to Almighty God that I will not allow the same.

The Gluttony of Josef Mengele
(The Angel of Death)

Mengele strutted along the line like a peacock picking
twins 2 by 2,
Selecting the wheat for his experiments throwing the
chaff away from view.

Little children robbed of innocence in an instance of a
knife,
Screams! Fall on deaf ears no thoughts for any life.

Experiments from a deranged mind of problems no
one cares,
The children devoured by animals in their many holes
and lairs.

Teeth ripped out and operations without anaesthetic,
Human kindness is forgotten any reason is pathetic.

On the run to Brazil with so many souls on beads,
A clear conscience has he that disturbs him not as he
reads.

Thrashing in the sea what fun he has a heart attack,
Wrestled from his mortal body the demons dragged
him back.

Why I Came

I came to Poland to see Auschwitz but I now wish I
never had,
That death looms all around me I'm not sleeping and
I'm sad.

I've looked into the abyss at Auschwitz 2 at Birkenau,
And heard the screams in terror that continue hour by
hour.

I've not slept since I got here and wake up in
selection lines,
Unaware of what they're saying and unable to read
the signs.

Other dreams have woke me as if I'm in work and
reading a list,
They are so vivid to me when they really don't exist.

Everyone's eyes are dead here when you look into their face,
With expressionless facial features that hold a ghostly trace.

It's like I am still dreaming and it's vivid to the end,
Or maybe I can't take it and its driven me round the bend.

I write these words in poetry form so you can take a look,
Then throw it from your mind like a line, sinker and a hook.

Don't come to this place in hell I beg you listen too,
Or you will suffer like me of the visions that I view.

If We Haven't Learned to Love.

The slaughter of the Jews was because of what they
were,
Apparently they had big crooked noses that made the
bigots stare.

The Nazi's came to power blaming them for every
woe,
And Hitler was a truth teller or did you never know.

The Germans came up with a solution to a problem
that wasn't there,
Then 11 million Jews and other races were killed it
really wasn't fair.

Worked to death or just slaughtered became their
only fate,
April 30th 1945 thank God it's an amazing date.

Hitler died in that besieged bunker without his hordes
and all alone,
No one would ever miss him and still don't know he's
gone.

So what have we all learned and what will the new dawn bring,

If we haven't learned to love each other then we haven't learned a thing.

Printed in Germany
by Amazon Distribution
GmbH, Leipzig